This...
...is about life.

Book III: Determine Your Outcome

a collection of poems from 1996-2016

by Randi Owens

...is about life.

Book III: Determine Your Outcome

*a collection of poems
from 1996-2016*

by Randi Owens

By: Randi Owens

Editor: Emily Autenrieth

Contributors:

Carlos Owens Jr
Maria Owens
Jose Owens
Xiomara Owens

Copyright ©
Printed in the U.S.A.
ISBN 978-0-9981443-2-0

First Edition 2016

For everyone...
Looking to the future

Table of contents

Introduction..xi

1996
Without You, There Would Be No Me 2
My Angel Maria 3

1997
Basketball Clones 6
Despair 7
Wish Upon a Starry Night 8
I Am Me 9

1999
Partnership 12

2000
Dream Awake 14

2001
Appreciation, I Thank You 16
The Forgotten 17
This Moment in Time 18
Little Did I Know 20
To Our Mother on Her Day 21

2003
The Walking Machine 24

2005
Is It Your "Nasty Day?" 26

Table of contents

2006
    The Value of an Education 28

2007
    The Chill That I Feel 30
    I Love You 31
    What Are My Limitations? 32

2008
    Possessed of Misery 34
    I Want… 35
    Get Right to the Point! 36
    CONCERN 37
    I Don't Have to Be in…to Be in 38

2009
    Irritation 40
    I'll Not Live Forever 41

2010
    Hurt Feelings 44
    Give Yourself a Wedgie 45
    Send Her an Angel (Maria) 47
    Grief 48
    Choice 49

2011
    Everyone Needs a Filter 52
    Who Am I…? 53
    She Chose to Hurt Me 54
    One More Chance 56
    There Are No Words 57

Table of contents

2012
Just Live 60
Waaa-Waaa...Get Over It 61
How to Help 62
Alcohol Abuse and Misuse Is Not the Answer 63
Choose to Live 64
The Observers 66
I'm Flying 67
The Ultimate in Leadership 68
Our Journey 69
Challenges 70
Don't Go to the Sad Corner 71
The Beat Up Old Heart 72

2013
It's ALL about You 76
Reaching Out 77
Fight to Survive 78
I Stand Alone 79
The Eagle 80
Please Look...and See Me 81
Once a Rock 82
Today Is a Good Day... 83
Aging 84
Mother's Day/Father's Day 86
Feeling on Top of the World 87
I Believe Success Is Earned 88
58: "Happy Birthday to You" 89
True and Everlasting Friendship 90
How Can We Ever Win? 92

Table of contents

2014
- My Heart Seeks...My Mind Incomplete 94
- What Makes You Smile? 95
- This Day Is Your Forever 96
- 9 Against 1 97
- I Can't Swim 98
- Feeling Uncomfortable 99
- Wait for It ... .100
- Give Back 101
- Self-Acceptance 102
- Sweet Ollie 103

2015
- Difficult to Explain 106
- Some Want Them 108
- Believe... 109
- The Bug 110
- You Are a Wonder 111
- Patience Resolves Much 112
- Who Am I That I Care? 113
- Share Your Thoughts 114

2016
- Woke Up Today 116
- Pain 117
- Naysay and Meaningless Chatter 119
- Longtime Friends 120
- Fishing 121
- Respect and Regard 122
- See, But Don't Be Seen 123
- Death Called 124

Table of contents

Feeling Pushed Over the Edge 126
No, Leo… 128
Black Man Running 130
Holding Hands.. 132
Winding Roads 133
Tennessee Sisters 134
North Pole Santa... 135
A Child's Prayer 136
Goodbye 137
Have All of the Answers... 138
It Was But A Whisper in My Ear 139
Travel to See Wonders of Nature 140
Shower Cry...141
Old But Useful 142
Smiles of Joy... 143
The Suburban, 1980 to 1997.. 144
There Is No Win, Only Hurt and Misery 145

Introduction

I wrote the following poems over a period of 20 years, beginning when I was venturing into mid-life with a focus on being a parent to four teenagers while settling into a variety of career changes over time. Those four teenagers have become beautiful adults, and each contributed poetry to this volume. The poems proved to be a valuable lifeline during a time when I felt unsure of my abilities as a wife, friend, mother, and grandmother tasked with the possibility of influencing the lives of those in my heart.

I believe poetry can provide therapeutic relief from worries and life's excess stressors. It invites readers to incorporate their thoughts and emotions into the words, creating the opportunity for temporary breaks from everyday life encounters. Through the poems, I learned that it is okay to be upset, smile, laugh, cry, and to simply live.

We can intertwine and cross what's real with fantasy ... if only just for that moment in time. I invite you to enter into the world of a woman willing to determine the outcome of her life without fear of the ending, bringing your personal thoughts and emotions with you during your journey.

1996

Without You, There Would Be No Me

God creates only one of us, and we are each unique
There are none like me, and when I'm gone, there'll still not be

There'll be none …
To do exactly as I have done

Should you truly wish to guide my troubled self
Please hear my silent plea for help

My behaviors and actions are not all that I am about
I implore you to see beyond what I do and sometimes what I shout

It is your commitment that encouraged me to look deep within
… where I rediscovered who I truly am and where I have been

You refused to give up long after I felt no one really cared
For your perseverance to see me through, I say thank you with my prayers

I once believed I had just cause to run, hide, or flee
Now, I am grateful to you because without you … there would be no me

My Angel Maria

My Angel you will always be
Determined and so special to me

I admire the way you carry yourself, so tall, with elegance and grace
I love the twinkle in your eyes when you succeed once you slow your pace

God has blessed you with a gift and you manage it well
Your father and I support you and believe you will not fail

Please forgive my occasional oversight when I think I know best
There are times when we argue that I realize you know more than I care to guess

I love you, Maria, and value you more than you'll ever know
Be strong for yourself as you strive to reach your goals

The things I've said are not hypocrisy, they come from the heart
My Angel Maria, I believe in you and have from the start

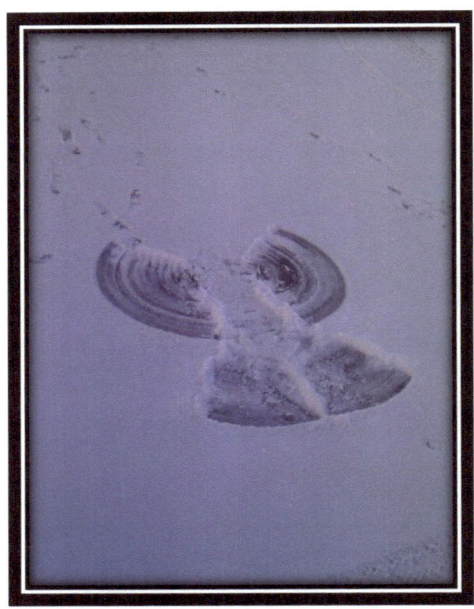

1997

Basketball Clones
by Maria O.

I can shoot through brick walls,
        hit nothin' but net
I'll drive down the lane doing 95
        Over, around, and through all that!
You can't stop the rain,
        'cause my shots are fallin' fast
I can pass the ROCK, I love to create
        Or I'll just take it myself--my game is fast-break!
You can't get by me, you can't shoot over this,
        Your game is child's play
        Here I am--Nope, think again,
        Now I'm behind you takin' it in!
Give me a step, I'll take you to the hole,
So you better step back 'cause you will get burned
I'm coming into your house and I'm not knockin'
So leave the door open or I'm huffin' and puffin'!
You think I'm play'n? This game is my life
        I live in my house,
        I eat in your kitchen,
        That ball is my sister,
        This net's my religion,
        My coach is my father
My shoes are my feet, my socks--my attire
        My skin's on the floor,
        My blood's on my shirt,
        My bruises are trophies
So - when you wanna visit? Come with a SPOON
'cause you better be ready to choke on some ball,
... and make room for seconds, 'cause that's not all!
If ya don't step aside, I'm takin' it in,
I come with my team and we leave with the win

Despair
by Maria O.

Here is where I lay my hand
Down upon this crisp, golden sand

Here is where I wish to be buried at last
The future looks dim, and I refuse to remain in the past

Away from the fire that will soon overcome the earth
Here is where I lay in despair as the earth forms its new fiery birth

Wish Upon a Starry Night
by Xiomara O.

I wished one night upon a star
... it suddenly fell close from skies afar

It shone bright and radiant as it fell in the distance
"... Hurry," I thought, "This is my chance"

Star light, star bright
... First star I see tonight

I wish I may, I wish I might
... find a love that will just take flight

A love so strong
... one could never break the bond

A love so intense
... It can't help but make sense

A love so pure
... it makes me feel secure

A wish for love that will not fail
My heart is open as I await my untold tale

I Am Me
by Xiomara O.

Before the grand jury I stand with years of denial
My acceptance of self is on trial
All eyes are on me
Awaiting my plea

As I slowly lift my head …
It took years for it to be said
In a world of such diversity
I find it so hard just to be "me"

With societal prejudice promoting injustice and shame
I can no longer deny the truth that I seek no fame
I have wanted so desperately to be true
To no one other than me … then later to you

Can I accept myself in the years to come?
Can you accept me for who I have become?
There is a world of wealth in acknowledging who I am and will someday be
There is a world of wealth in recognizing who I will become as I accept me

I will drown in my own wealth of self unless I can feel free
To express myself and be who I choose to be
I shift my weight and look into their eyes
For once in my life I'm sure of my demise

I clear my throat
And begin to devote
My past thoughts and memories
Into positive energy

I look at my audience, and begin to speak as I smile with glee
I am human; I am female; I am gay; I am me

1999

Partnership

When your partner is loyal and knows what to do
Look for the good that is between you

Does it really matter that he left the seat up?
Does it really matter that she forgot to flush?

Is it important that your partner doesn't speak loud enough for you to hear?
The beauty lies in knowing the confidence each shares, without thought or fear

Why is it so frustrating when your partner has incomplete chores as you've described?
Think instead of the fun activities the two of you are missing while you live and thrive

You each could have had someone else but instead made the best selection
Learn to appreciate and feel thankful for your blessed partnership connection

Partner with a smile from one day to the next as you live and have fun
This creates an opportunity for a lasting relationship, for many years to come

2000

Dream Awake

In the beginning, it's dark and gloomy as I stumble, trip, and sometimes fall
I struggle on because there's a light at the end of the hall

The trials and tribulations astound me
There are restraining bonds of which I cannot see

I find myself wondering what it is that I should do
Pick up where I left off … or start something new

The questions are abundant, my mind is unsure
Will there be an ending, or is there simply no cure?

2001

Appreciation, I Thank You

You are one-of-a-kind
You're always on my mind

When I'm with you, my heart does a double take
My clumsiness is gone and I make few mistakes

You make me glow when all seems dim
You are the light which puts shine to this gem

Without you, I would not be
Most of all, I love you for loving and appreciating me

The Forgotten

Acknowledged and appeased, it feels good to have a cause
Loss of self occurs rapidly when you are no longer the boss

Pride is a forgotten entity when reality sets in
You believe yourself alone as your will refuses to bend

There are no lasting sites to view as you walk away
The time to watch the sunset has passed, and tomorrow starts a new day

Dreams do come true, you think, and the future looks bright
The changes of life are inevitable, but don't quit without a fight

Memories begin to flood your mind as you seek solitude
There is no place to hide as survival becomes the only rule

Knowledge is your weapon as patience is your guide
Seek comfort in your wisdom, lest you be forgotten before you die

This Moment in Time
by Jose O.

This is the story of our first date
Some say that this moment just had to be fate

These feelings I felt, I'll try to describe
The thoughts that I had, thoughts that I couldn't hide

How I made it through, I'll never know
But for the first few moments, I sure put on a good show

The fear that held onto me refused to let go
This is the story I want you to know

I stepped out of my car, all confident and clean
I continued to walk, the whole time losing steam

My excitement grew fast until it was fear
All for the mere fact that you were so near

Now onto the porch my heart fluttering about
A lump in my throat, mouth dry as a drought

As I knocked on the door
... my feet froze to the floor

I can't move, I can't breathe!
... Oh God, help me, please!

(continued...)

(This Moment in Time)

Time slows
… as the fear in me grows

Footsteps … so delicate, so light …
The door opens! The peak of my fright!

And there you are, pretty smile and all
You notice the flowers I hold as I stand there in awe

With the most beautiful thanks, the most precious sound
Every word that you speak lifts my feet off the ground

The fear in me is gone as I gaze into your eyes
So innocent, so pure, untouched by harsh lies

As you place your hand into mine, I realize it's time
Let's get on with this date, for everything is fine

This moment was fate, this moment in time

Little Did I Know
by Jose O.

Little did I know that I would fall in love
Little did I know I would be sent a beautiful angel from above

Little did I know someone would love me for dear, imperfect me
Little did I know that in your arms is the only place I would want to be

Little did I know that my world could be so bright
Little did I know that kissing someone could feel so right

Little did I know we were both wishing upon the same mystical star in the sky
Little did I know you were to be the person I want to be with from now
    until the day I die

Little did I know I would meet my soul mate
Little did I know ...

Little did I know ... it was fate

To Our Mother on Her Day
by Xiomara O.

I say to so many people when they tell me how much alike are we ...
"Let me show you the true Randi," the one they fail to see

The numerous greetings are met with a smile of perfect pearls
Every time, as though it's been years since she's seen her baby girl

The dark of her eyes are silently revealing memories of many years
The ever-shining sparkle, reminiscent of matching us all tear for tear

I will admit and claim responsibility for some of the hairs gone white
From years of "patience is a virtue" and "you're stronger if you don't fight"

The strength contained is virtually unfathomable, in the small frame
    of my mother's build
From giving us direction when we lacked the will

This is to you, Mom, on your day,
For giving us strength all along the way

For being my mother when it was hard to be my friend
And for being my friend when, as a mother, you felt you would never win

This is to you, Mom, on your day
For giving us strength all along the way

2003

The Walking Machine

The walking machine chose a long path with hills and valleys
She liked to walk and share her joy with friends and family

The walks were pretty fast and she never saw as she went around the bend …
That her walking partners were behind and trying to catch their second wind

The walking machine found it hard to find anyone willing to go on a walk
They all made excuses because her rapid pace left them unable to talk

She attempted to slow down and walk everyone else's speed
But found it difficult to retain the pace and meet her own needs

She walked alone many days, enjoying nature's view along the way
Walking is one of her favorite pastimes, and doing it alone is okay

2005

Is It Your "Nasty Day?"

When someone else is having a bad day and taking it out on you
Never allow their ugly behavior to make you ugly too

What's wrong with me, you say ... that negative energies seem to be concentrated
  in my direction?
Why does something have to be wrong with you? Choose to go around them
  and make a better selection.

Use your inner strength to combat the outer turmoil and decay
Hold your head up high as you keep distress and distraught at bay

Surround yourself with positive thoughts and feelings that you believe possible and true
Remember, there is so much more to life than the "nasty" negatives others direct at you

No, you aren't alone in your perceived semblance of misery, pain, and woe
Yes, there exist people who derive joy from bringing others low

Are you the master in control of your life, steering your ship through troubled waters
  during stormy nights?
The decision to survive and thrive is yours alone--should "nasty" take control
  and keep away your light?

Seek the sunshine outside of the gloom if you are to succeed
To weep and cry are not options if you are to keep your spirit free

Is it your "nasty day" or is it for someone else? I say, you'll have to decide
As for me, I have joy in my heart and a smile on my face as I step into the rain outside

2006

The Value of an Education

I'll get a job at an establishment that doesn't require an education to perform
I'll do what it takes for me to get by, and I'll not fret over the norm

"That'll be $2.49 for your order to go"
"Where's my change, you nitwit? Are you stupid or just plain slow?"

"I gave you a five dollar bill and as change, you returned two"
"I apologize for the error, I'll get the remaining dollar change you're due"

That job wasn't for me, there are plenty of other things I can do to pay bills …
I've always wanted to work with children and help them learn new skills

This job is a lot of fun, there aren't very many responsibilities to uphold
I watch the children, feed them, and in their young lives, play a positive role

"The medication you gave that child was not for them to take!
Didn't you read the name on the label? How could you make such a mistake?"

I guess I was lucky that time, the parents didn't press charges against me
My friend's father needs a secretary, the work is minimal, and it pays a good salary

But there was a lot of typing and I couldn't concentrate
The misspelled words and paragraph displacements created havoc and debate

Something is missing, I'm depressed and often sad
My dreams have all wilted and my life is worse than bad

I feel I am ready for the education I initially refused to endure
I know it won't be easy and of the future I am unsure

I do know that if I but try, I'll have a better chance to survive
It feels good to make a decision … to choose … to be alive

The value of an education cannot be over emphasized
    as a personal choice
Education is the answer to making change and providing voice

2007

The Chill That I Feel

The chill that I feel is not from what you say
The chill that I feel will not let me go astray

The chill that I feel is a chill to the bone
The chill that I feel makes me feel all alone

The chill that I feel reaches deep into my soul
The chill that I feel makes me feel old

The chill that I feel has years to suppress
---the pain that I experience inside my chest

I Love You

A simple statement I speak from my heart
I feel better with you than when we are apart

This three-word statement to give or to take
Is meaningful to some and, to others, a mistake

What does it really mean, to thine heart be true--
What does it really mean, this "I Love You?"

When I wake in the morning to discover you there
Does it mean I love you because I know you care?

What does it mean when I feel I have not been heard?
What does it mean when there is little emotion to the word?

L-O-V-E is beautiful, meaning to be thoughtful and giving, with goodness in kind
For me to say "I Love You" is to say I feel connected to your heart and mind

I Love You should be spoken with gentle sincerity as it awakens the heart from slumber
It should be shouted at the top of your lungs with volume and emotional thunder

I often question that which I do not understand
… Is love to be gained and lost on demand?

Sometimes I think of love as a "lost and found" kit of surprise
But mostly I think of love as a special thought reserved in a beautiful disguise

What Are My Limitations?

Dare I limit myself or seek to achieve more
Life is better than it was before

I can allow others to stay my heart and mind
Or I can accept that only I limit myself in time

What are my limitations ... do they exist?
Not if I decide to follow through and persist

Dreams are precious and convey a future at hand
I listen closely and I'm confident in my desire to expand

My destination is my own and the outcome firm
There are no limitations as long as I choose to learn

Limitations within reason, I am limited only by choice
They don't have to exist as long as I have voice

What are my limitations? I say there are none
We often limit ourselves, at times before we have begun

2008

Possessed of Misery

What could have happened in someone's life to make them so unsound?
They look at you as though, because you're alive, it makes them want to drown

It is quite a challenge to keep your face stern and unforgiving
It requires less muscle action to smile than to keep your smile hidden

Misery reforms your face and keeps others at bay
The look says, "I'll make you unhappy, unless I am getting my way"

Their satisfaction in the presence of others is rare as they second-guess intentions
They thrive on making others miserable as they strengthen their desire for contention

Possessed of misery prohibits the body's need to relax
--emits an aura of discontent while stifling a kindness of heart
Possessed of misery leaves the owner rigid and tense
--limiting positive interaction while keeping them worlds apart

It is as though they are depressed from lack of joy and peace
How can anyone become whole as a person until the upheavals cease?

Anyone can be happy, smile, and receive pleasure simply from watching the joys of others
Instead, with misery possessed, there are those that watch for an opportunity to frown, welcoming it
Like a long-lost lover

I Want...

I want to live
Why must I die?
I want to be happy
Why must I cry?

I want to smile--often
 Why must I be sad?
I want to be good
Why must I be bad?

I want to succeed
Why must I doubt that I can?
I want to be debt-free
Why must I spend on demand?

I want to enjoy my job
Why must I "make" myself go through the door?
I want to retire and do something FUN
Why must I drag it out while feeling bored?

I want to be well and healthy
Why must I be slowed and in pain?
I want to achieve all of my goals
Why must I negate all that I've gained?

Get Right to the Point!

I don't mean to be rude and I have no desire to be cruel
Our time is limited and discussion vital, and there are few rules

Patience is necessary, opportunity to share is sought
Courtesy is welcomed and opinions provoke thought

Everyone is entitled to present their view over time
Getting right to the point negates the need to be refined

Don't think I'm heartless or selfish in form
To me, "getting right to the point" is my norm

I have no desire to leave anyone out
Please speak up, even if you have to shout

I value your knowledge, years of wisdom, experience, and all you've taught
Sometimes it's best for me to slow, look around, and regroup my thoughts

Get right to the point isn't an intention, instead it's a communication style
I look forward to learning from your cache of mind-boggling "lessons learned" files

CONCERN

We must learn to live with ourselves before living or working with others
These are lessons learned early on, from our fathers and mothers

CONCERN:
Think before you speak
Words are not easily recalled once spoken, and the hurt can run deep

CONCERN:
I know my job and in conversing with you
... I now have an idea of what I need to do

CONCERN:
For the knowledge I am grasping I feel grateful to the fates
For the worthwhile endeavors I look forward to a time to celebrate

CONCERN:
Know me and respect me
... for who I am, not as you wish me to be

COMPLAINT:
Life is short: Gripes and concerns are often party to human nature's decline
You can choose to make things better or accept the group cooperation as aligned

If it can be fixed and you want it, you fix it
... if not, make adjustments to live with it

I Don't Have to Be in...to Be in...

I walk into the room and the whispers begin
I want to turn and leave but refuse to give in

I'm reminded that they're nice people but they aren't my friends
I have to stop wearing my heart on my sleeve and letting their actions offend

I don't have to be in ... to be in, and I accept being left out
They like each other's company and the trips they talk and banter about

The more I look for the positive, I genuinely smile at their clever quips
... and at how pleased everyone is with their social weekend trips

I choose to be happy for their gatherings and close companionship
I choose to respect their annual events of fun and ignore any insensitive slips

Work is often a place where employees act like a dysfunctional family
Similar to sibling rivalries, gossip, and passive/aggressive tendencies

No, I don't have to be in ... to be in ... and it's really alright
I like what I do at work and it's not such a distressing plight

2009

Irritation

Is it me, or do I irritate others simply by being there?
Is it me, or does my presence set off alarms everywhere?

I limit my words, assess my approach, and watch my step
And yet I'm looked at with contempt should I dare to seek help

What's this phenomenon prompting such malice and desire to beat me down?
Why not use more energy to offer kindness, or words to make you happy and not frown?

I often wonder, is it me? ... or maybe they're having a bad day
I allow their response to dampen my joy as I turn and walk away

Is it me, or do I irritate others simply by being there, looking vulnerable and incomplete?
What should I do as I note their behaviors, finding no desire for a negative response
    or requite?

I believe that to respond in turn is to give away personal power and control
I accept this as my life and the ill treatment of anyone else is not allowed to take hold

Why must I believe it is me or that I've done anything wrong to cause such cruel intent?
When will I accept that everyone has "attitude," and invariably exercise their right to vent?

I no longer choose to second-guess or view it as a concern when others' lives get out of hand
There will always be those placing their troubles on someone else simply because they can

I'll Not Live Forever

Let not my death be in vain
Find joy in the memories beyond the pain

I am complete in the love I feel
My mind is clear, my wounds are healed

With my arms held wide, I embrace you all
It is your beauty and acceptance that I recall

What a blessing to have lived among you freely
I feel there is no place in the world I'd rather be

There is time still to weep for the loss of my life
I'd rather you celebrate with smiles and tears of me as a mother and wife

I love you all and I don't want to go, "Wow, what a wild ride"
I did things I never thought I'd do in life before I died

Let not my death be in vain
Find joy in the memories beyond the pain

I am complete in the love that I feel
My mind is clear, my wounds are healed

My arms held wide, I embrace you all
It's your beauty and acceptance I see as I fall

What a Blessing I have lived amongst you free
There's no one in the world that's luckier than me

2010

Hurt Feelings

My feelings are hurt and I don't understand
… why he waddled up my note and threw it in the trash can

I felt confused and lost as if he'd taken away my spark
I withheld my emotions as he walked away into the dark

I asked myself why, when I'm feeling good and healthy
… would someone come along and take that away from me?

My thoughts were of love as I wrote with feelings that were strong
I tried to capture that love not realizing I'd done anything wrong

But as he read and I watched him frown and not respond
I had to rethink my thoughts about what I had done

Maybe he'd had a bad day and brought it home
What he did hurt so bad until I just wanted to be left alone

Give Yourself a Wedgie

You wake in the morning feeling out of sorts
Can't decide whether to wear panties or undershorts

Already frustrated with the day that is yet to begin
Angry at your peers, both the ladies and the men

Your clothes are wrinkled and your shoes have spots
Choose the suit with the blue polka dots

The mirror reveals that your hair will offend
You're running late--will this day never end?

Breakfast is not an option as your stomach makes sounds
You run down the stairs and your heart begins to pound

Out the front door with keys in hand
The tank is near empty, you don't understand

The day appears long, filled with strange looks and smiles
Once it ends, there is the drive home and the lonely miles

You run out of gas and the station is far, far away
The rickety truck that stops to offer help makes you want to fall to your knees and pray

The return trip is silent and you're left at the off ramp with your gas can
The driver pulls away laughing out loud as you assess your day and how it began

You look down at your clothes, noting the blue polka dot jacket and
    the red striped slacks
You remember the looks throughout the day and the laughter behind your back

(continued...)

(Give Yourself a Wedgie)

You look closely at your shoes, seeing their mismatched colors, one dark gray
    and one blue
The trip to the car becomes one of personal insight as you view yourself anew

As you sit in the car looking in the mirror, thinking of the long drive home and
    of the long miles
You are appalled at the image of your never-brushed yellow teeth as you smile

Apparently, you forgot to brush your teeth during the mad dash out
You cry upon recalling the laughter during the day, finally understanding
    what it was about

As you open the bedroom door and begin to undress
… give yourself a wedgie and laugh loudly at your Friday the 13th mess

Send Her an Angel (Maria)

Send her an angel, someone that is big, bold, and strong
Send her an angel, someone to convince her she's done nothing wrong

Send her an angel, someone to help sort the pieces to her puzzle of life
Send her an angel, someone to help make everything alright

Send her an angel, someone who stays steady as she grows strong
Send her an angel, someone to take her places she's never gone

Send her an angel, someone with beautiful foresight
Send her an angel, someone to walk beside her in battle as she wins the fight

Send her an angel, I know you have someone in mind
Send her an angel, someone wonderful and kind

Send her an angel, she deserves one as her life unfolds
Send her an angel, someone to fulfill her beautiful heart of gold

Send her an angel, someone to see through to her heart
Send her an angel, someone to guide her from the start

Send her an angel, someone you've chosen through your grace
Send her an angel, someone to tell her it's never too late

Send her an angel, someone to see the beauty that she holds
Send her an angel, someone with whom she can grow old

Send her an angel, to you my God I pray
Send her an angel, someone that by her side they will always stay

SEND HER AN ANGEL!

Grief

I hurt inside and I don't know what to say
I run to my room with my toys and begin to play

Putting my pain aside, somehow I remember the cookies Grandma and I would bake
Just as the train whistle blows, I think, "There's the train we would often take"

Sometimes I'd cry myself to sleep at night
The memories so strong, I'd want to take flight

My mom said I should smile because everything will be okay
I'd look at her and think, "With Grandma gone, I feel my heart has been taken away"

One day, my mom showed me a picture where I was missing my two front teeth
It reminded me of my grandma placing hers in a glass before going to sleep

I started to smile at the many fond memories I had
… of my grandma and me before she died, leaving me deeply sad

I no longer focused on the grief and the pain as I grew to be a man
Instead I recalled the wisdom and gave thanks for my grandma's gentle hands

Those fond memories got me through the months and years, helping me to grow strong
I share them with my children as we smile about my childhood with Grandma long gone

Choice

I'm told I live in a world full of possibilities and hope
When often on the news it's about crime, death, and dope

Everyone insists that I succeed
That I follow the rules and do good deeds

I have seen beggars, drunks, and the homeless in need
Could this be eliminated, were there less greed?

My parents say I'm blessed, intelligent, and bright
They say I'll be among those to make things right

My heart is willing, and my mind is strong
I have to believe that I'm not alone

The future world is what I make it for me
I can choose to be chained or I can choose to be free

2011

Everyone Needs a Filter

A filter withstands the heartache, ugliness, and words profane
It is someone with much to lose and nothing to gain

A filter is patient, withholding tongue and thought
Looking the other way, knowing they are criticized if they talk

The filter is kind of spirit with a heart that's open and fair
They're helpful through the difficult times, always being aware

A filter takes the verbal abuse, wanting others to be seen as being true
Once the verbal rants are complete, the fallout is mostly through

A filter listens, helping those they love to talk it out with them
Believing they're overworked and stressed, making for their upset on a whim

As a filter, there's oftentimes little acceptance of their comments
A filter tends to quietly listen as they calmly minimize the offense

A filter affords the opportunity to see options at hand
Without a filter, the complainants often make harsh demands

Everyone needs a filter to help monitor their emotions
With a filter, there's a chance for an increase in discipline and devotion

Who Am I...?

I am nobody ... I am seen and yet unseen
I stand tall, and yet continue to lean

Who am I ... I am often heard and yet remain unheard
I am included and yet often left out without a word

Who am I ... Invisible and yet solid mass
I know myself well and yet not well enough, leaving me an outcast

Who am I ... a bright light seen from afar awaiting someone's call
But when in close proximity, I'm nobody and not seen at all

No one cares for what I feel to share
Nor feels for what I dare to care

I am found, but was never lost
I hold back, wanting to reach out at all costs

Is it okay to hurt my feelings because I lack response?
Perhaps I have no feelings to hurt ... although I believe I did once

Reinforce your pretense for concern of my needs
As your concern for my needs are a reinforced pretense to justify your deeds

Who am I ... and can nobody become somebody?
Who are you ...? I want to be somebody but I'm nobody!

Who am I ... and who do I want to be? I want to be somebody!
Nobody ever receives respect, but I want somebody to respect me

Somebody is a sure bet, nobody is ignored and left outside alone
Somebody is complemented and brought into the home

Nobody is seen while in the front row
Somebody is never missed even when getting up to go

Who am I ... and who do I want to be?
I am Somebody and there's nobody else quite like me, but me

She Chose to Hurt Me

I felt discomfort with the sharp pains in my chest
I understood my best friend's concern and her distress

My time with her was interrupted by my heart disease
I didn't want to go to the clinic, but the discomfort didn't cease

As I was checked in, I felt a distinct unease
I wanted to tell my friend, "Don't leave me, please"

I told the nurse of my small veins and that they tend to roll
She said, "The attending nurse setting the IV will be told"

I listened to my friend's small talk and reassurance for my care
I felt grateful to God that for me, she was there

The delay was but a small reprieve
Our discussion was interrupted as she was told to leave

The attending nurse arrived and closed the door
Immediately, I felt chilled to my core

She told my friend she'd be told when to return to my side
The look on her face made me want to run and hide

I repeated that my veins are small and tend to roll as she gloved her hands
She said she'd been informed and that she did understand

With the first jab of the needle, I flinched and looked away
I bit my tongue, the tears flowing while she fished for the vein that rolled astray

I cried out in pain as I was jabbed in the hand
She revealed no remorse for causing pain as she jabbed me again

Not a word was spoken as she plied the needle twice more
It was unbearable and I screamed, but no one came to the door

(continued...)

(She Chose to Hurt Me)

Later, I wondered why no one came to rescue me
There should never have been that much pain for placement of an IV

My arm was bruised and my tears flowed free
She never said a word as she walked away from me

My friend reentered the room with her emotions on her face
I desperately wanted her to take me away from that place

She shared how much she'd wanted to return to the room to be by my bed
But deferred to the nurse's request to stay out instead

I looked at my friend and said, "Please never bring me here again
… Take me someplace else, as far away as you can"

The doctor came in and we discussed my heart stents and concerns
I thanked him with a promise to visit my cardiologist upon my return

I cringed at the idea of remaining in their facility
They had to have heard my outcry, and yet no one came to see

I'd never experienced anything like my treatment by that nurse before or since that day
She was cold, cruel, sadistic, and inconsiderate of my pain while helplessly I lay

The trauma is memorable, but I can't recall her face
Perhaps that's a blessing as the recall of the incident still makes my heart race

She chose to hurt me in her profession of compassion and care
She chose to hurt me and to become the subject of my nightmares

I choose not to judge all nurses by her actions and disgrace
I choose to recall the ones that treated me with compassion on their face

I remember the many nurses with tears held back in their eyes
They are my true heroes as their care of me was open and without disguise

I choose not to allow the behavior of one to taint what the others do
I'm grateful to my good nurses and I appreciate all of you

One More Chance

My eyes see you as you are today
My heart sees you as you were when I chose to leave rather than stay

I recall when I asked you to be my bride
The crushing feeling when your answer of "No" hurt my bruised pride

The havoc and destruction I sought in part
In an effort to command my broken heart

Distance became my friend and a lie
With you in my heart, there were times I felt I wanted to die

My strength and perseverance allowed me to go on
You were never forgotten, but I chose not to be alone

With you as the love of my heart, I wed the love of my life
Such memories I have to have loved so deeply twice

It was a sad day when the mother of my children … my precious wife
Was claimed by death, leaving my heart shattered yet again in my life

I know I am blessed to have found you again
Giving me one more chance to ask you for your hand

Our remaining years together, my angel, are pure bliss
And I look forward to committing to the years we have missed

There Are No Words

When connections are good, smile, you don't need me--you have God, and he won't abort
When connections are not so good, smile, you have God--I'm here for backup and support

The memories keep you strong and focused on today
The tears are reminders that things don't always go your way

Though there were times of togetherness when we were strained
I sometimes thought you should go when I really wanted you to remain

We didn't always see eye to eye
Yet, it is my love for you that makes me cry

Perfection sought is nothing more than a word in place
Seldom as meaningful and permanent as true acts of grace

Realization has yet to settle that you are no longer here to see
Although it helps knowing that you are now pain-free

My hurt is real and my heart bleeds for you with death's claim
I recall our many encounters resulting in the life experiences we gained

Our time together has come to an end much too fast
The present allows me to conjure up memories of the past

My thoughts of who we were are here to stay
Nothing we shared will ever wither, decay, or go away

I miss you my dear heart …
And for that, there are no words strong enough to impart

2012

Just Live

Life changes are many, with no end in sight
If you are to survive, then choose to fight

One can accept that over which we have limited control
And live a healthy life as we grow old

There is an opportunity to whine and regret the aging process as grim
Perhaps the wiser role is to accept the change, enjoy life, and act on a whim

Relearn yourself and note all that you can do
Limit the things that no longer define you

There remains happiness and joy from some memories of your past
Allow their presence to strengthen you as a new die is cast

Make use of diet, exercise, and friends at large
Look forward to life changes and choose to take charge

Get up and move, do something other than stand still
Excuses are easy to acquire, but like cancer, they can kill

Think of what you can accomplish and less of things out of reach
With your life experience, there is much you can teach

Waaa-Waaa...Get Over It

Poor me, I am in pain and no one understands
I cannot explain my body's demands

Is it fair to talk about it to my friends?
They can't help me fix the problem or ensure that I mend

My doctor is thoughtful and responds with care
Even he appears to limit his understanding to be fair

Medication, diet, exercise, and personal thoughts
Help to manage the discomfort and daily onslaught

I find it easier to resort to self-pity at times
Until I see and hear of others with a worst diagnosis than mine

I live with something that allows for good days and bad
I struggle with limitations and miss the good days I once had

This isn't a death sentence, although that will someday arrive
There remains time to achieve goals and be thankful that I am alive

I accept that when feeling at a loss I don't always use my wit
I need to stop whining and just say, "Waaa-waaa, now get over it"

How to Help

Ask yourself, "Do they want my help, and will it make a difference to them?"
Will forcing yourself to do something result in you being out on a limb?

Never lose sight of the fact that this isn't about you
When your offer to help is on the table, it's about what they need to do

Perhaps they enjoy themselves just as they are today
Your assumptions of their need for help may simply get in their way

You can overreact and overwhelm with offers to assist
Many are strengthened by their experience and not pleased when you persist

Determine if you will always be in their lives and at their disposal
If the answer is no, now where do you go with your help proposal?

How to help with an offer of guidance, ideas, and support
Be patient and listen thoughtfully to their retort

There will be willing recipients of a sincere request for help
Less anxious to take over their life when they have yet to take the first step

Defer to them as they assess their ability to follow through
Be encouraging, open, and honest when it is required of you

Alcohol Abuse and Misuse Is Not the Answer

Need a drink to get through the day
Order of thinking keeps running astray

Attempt to formulate a thought still unclear
Perhaps the process requires another beer

Have trouble walking, the path is not straight
A glass of wine ensures the struggle will abate

Head is spinning and feels like a balloon
Have a single shot of liquor to ease the way until noon

Eyes are bloodshot and the day too bright
Looking forward to a mixed drink to clear eyesight

Want to relax but feel jittery and upset
Plan to meet friends later and win the drinking bet

No desire to eat, everything tastes funny
Running low on funds, too drunk to earn money

Emotional and physical discomfort appears to drive one insane
Additional consumption will temporarily negate the pain

Alcohol is not the answer, or so it is told
Yet when consumed, many feel 10 feet tall and extremely bold

What a loss those memories set aside from the mind
Why not a controlled casual drink versus the many that suppress time?

The opportunity to think, see, taste, and walk without support is a gain
Allowing personal respect for oneself in order to utilize the strength needed
    to thy life sustain

Choose to Live

Cutting to ease the pain of others' dislike and words of scorn
Versus acceptance of this beautiful, unblemished shell into which you were born

Burning to numb the pain of sexual attacks by family members, strangers, and friends
Versus acceptance of help to get your life on track and allow your healing to begin

Pills to black out while escaping reality when you no longer want to exist
Versus calling on those you trust to convince you that, in death, there's life you will miss

Abundance of substance use for acceptance and to please
Versus clarity of mind experienced in order to avoid such misdeeds

Threaten self-harm or commit suicide to draw attention to struggles as defined
Versus communicating ill thoughts to those that want you to heal, succeed, and shine

Engage in self-destructive behaviors where there is little chance to survive
Acknowledge the permanence of death; paralyzed, injured; and choose to remain alive

Become physically or verbally abusive to others and threaten death when you disagree
Or seek help upon realizing your possessive, angry, and disconcerting tendencies

Consider becoming a martyr that others may later recall
Or understand that your irreplaceable absence does not fix their problems at all

Choose life when irrational thoughts appear, making it easier to die or suicide attempt
Or allow the world at large to be privy to your precious developing talents

Does suicide or attempts make a statement to your cause or provide a loud shout?
Reconsider your options by choosing life and survival over self- doubt

(continued...)

(Choose to Live)

Many may view your desire to follow through as selfish, thoughtless, and unkind
With access to weapons when distraught, there's little consideration
    for those left behind

The determination and willingness to succeed has no age as foretold
A single solution for all would never be a goal

Unique as we are, inner strength is a must
Relief of pain by suicide is not a viable option to trust

Choose to live, even knowing the future may be disappointing and tough
Your spark of life has much to offer to those on the receiving end and is
    more than enough

Choose to live, allowing others through you to want to survive
You never know whom you'll influence or how by encountering them,
    you will change their lives

Choose to live, accepting that death does provide an ending
Seek to lighten your spirit as you challenge life's new beginnings

The Observers

When attending an event alone
Invisibility is often prone

Therefore, partnering with someone when asked
May prove an impossible task

Some people arrive with peers they know
Others interact with those whose similarities show

Don't think they're purposely being cruel
So much as people tend to follow their innate rules

Once eye contact is made with several in the group that's there
Acknowledge the avoidance as a discomfort they share

It can be a distant assessment without thought or choice
There's often a tendency to analyze life via observation without voice

Observe life around you and the communication it entails
Judge not the finality as interactions are unveiled

The Observers frequently become lost in a crowded settings flow
Few are aware of their presence as they watch individuals come and go

I'm Flying

I'm flying... I'm flying and it feels like fun
I'm flying... I'm flying and it is better than going for a run

I'm flying....I'm flying and I'm on the go
I'm flying... I'm flying and moving fast, not slow

I'm flying... I'm flying and no one's in my way
I'm flying... I'm flying and it's such a beautiful day

I'm flying... I'm flying and I'm full of hope
I'm flying... I'm flying and I'm learning to cope

I'm flying....I'm flying watching the clouds as I lie
I'm flying... I'm flying seeing my life before me as I fly

I'm flying... I'm flying and the sky is blue and clear
I'm flying... I'm flying and I often wish you were here

I'm flying... I'm flying and my wings are full of grace
I'm flying... I'm flying and up here I don't feel out of place

I'm flying... I'm flying and I feel secure within myself
I'm flying... I'm flying as if I'm the only one left

I'm flying... I'm flying as I stretch out my winged arms
I'm flying... I'm flying and when you see me, don't become alarmed

I'm flying... I'm flying and it makes me feel unique
I'm flying... I'm flying and at last I feel complete

The Ultimate in Leadership

You set out on this journey knowing it would not be easy to succeed
When you are a trailblazer, you find balance if you are to do what you need

There are many willing to offer support while others cause you grief
You hold your head high as you soldier through, taking what you can in relief

They cry out as they look to you for guidance and a semblance of peace of mind
Many sense that you understand their struggles and that to them you are not blind

It is your unfailing wisdom and refusal to give in that helps in your advance
Your acceptance of difficulties and challenges make you worthy of another chance

The gray hair seemed to come to you overnight
Your worries no longer hidden, but shown in plain sight

It's harder than you originally believed, but you remained strong when criticized
You refused to give up on the people, taking their judgment of you in stride

The battle was in progress long before you accepted the office for two terms
You were willing to put your life on the line to share the many lessons learned

The poor are truly getting poorer as more is taken away
Many wealthy seek to secure their lives as their humanity goes on display

The middle class bears the burdens and the weight of the American dream
The challenges before us today are as great and vast as an ocean to a small stream

Each has natural barriers allowing them to provide for the lives in their care
The barriers allow us to assess what's beneath the surface that is beautiful and rare

We exert precious energy while the disagreements continue on every front
The peace we say we seek is one we forever tend to hunt

The years you serve your country will be recalled with pride and regret
Never forget that you served with wisdom of heart and endeavored to do your best

As I watch you, I understand your grace and that perfection was never your intent
I feel pride in knowing that you meet your challenges with strength and confidence

A President to Be Remembered!

Our Journey

As members of God's community, there are many stages to our journeys
    in the life that we lead
We face the challenges encountered and continue to cheer each other on with glee

We encourage ourselves as we accept encouragement from family and friends
Life is like cleaning and healing as we move through life's journey, purging
    as we mend

We recognize our wish for things to be different as we strive to succeed and not fail
We acknowledge the reality of life: it is not always fair, but neither is it a fairytale

We accept that life won't always begin or end as we would like with a certainty
We wash away the pains and burdens that we bear in an effort to feel free

As we quietly look into the beauty of the light so full of God's loving care
Our flowing tears remind us of the challenges to come and that we are not there

From day to day, week to week, and year to year we dare to dream and pray
We gradually release our burdens to God and realize that he's here to stay

We quench our thirst for salvation and are gracious in our praise to God
    for all he has done,
We accept that in our journey there are many, of which we are but one

Challenges

There is darkness all around me and I'm afraid to make a sound
I seek the comfort of my mother's arms, but she's nowhere to be found

The desire to scream and cry out loud almost overwhelm me
Something from within creates a calm that allows me to see

I lost a part of me when my mother and father passed away
My childhood was too serious, with little time for play

I found that I am capable and willing to learn to be free
of the demons from the past that continued to haunt me

There have been many trials and tribulations and I pray to be strong
I make decisions that are right and ask forgiveness for the wrong

The present is so trying and sometimes the pain is great
I know that should I falter, my life is forfeited to fate

There's no place to hide and no longer can I run
The demons are behind me and I must let my life move on

Faith is real, and it helps to know I should always hold it close
It's through faith I'll flourish in my future with fewer doubts than most

I can't seem to thrive without a constant challenge of deed
Inner turmoil works to keep me bound to be responsible for those in need

Don't Go to the Sad Corner

Don't go to the sad corner, where it's dark with despair
Open up the door so that you can get some fresh air

Don't go to the sad corner, where you kneel and face the wall when caught
Think about the consequence before you're found to be at fault

Go out into the sunshine and smile into the breeze
Be happy for the day as you gather up the leaves

Chase after a butterfly and laugh while you play
No, don't go to the sad corner, at least not today

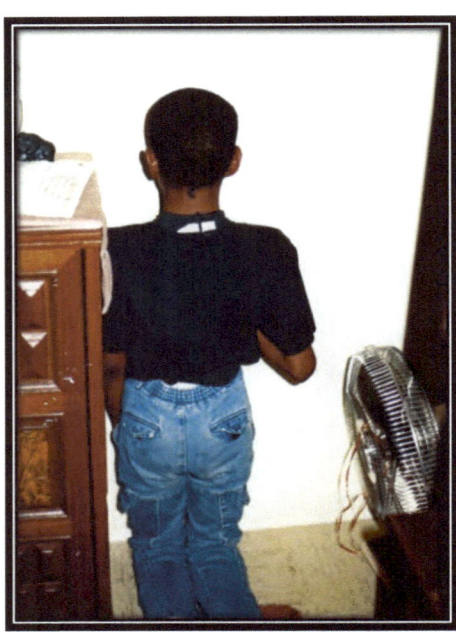 

The Beat Up Old Heart

Like the engine to an old 55 Chevy, there's much work to be done
This heart has miles beyond measure, but it still runs

It's been driven to the point of stopping, providing needed transportation and fun
It struggles to keep going as it is determined to get the job done

If it could talk, mere words could never convey the full story
It remains humble and dignified in all of its worn glory

There were days when the start was slow and the pain great
But it was sheer determination that kept it from being late

The abuse it withstood, few could command
And there it was, pushing forward without demand

There was no room for complaints with so much to be done
There was a plea for it not to stop because the kids needed to have fun

Remember the events of cheerleading, baseball, football, and track
How we've always managed to get there and back

No one wants what they love to struggle in vain
It's important to stay focused on the straight and narrow traveling lanes

The rumbling noise and tough starts indicating the possible end
Were vivid reminders that without a gentle tug, you wouldn't get around the bend

Stoic and beautiful, though damaged and rewired
There was no slowing even when it tired

(continued...)

(The Beat Up Old Heart)

The rhythm was strong and steady through two jobs, sometimes three
Although the occasional hard thumps were heard, there were only a few leaks

There were tears and prayers to take one step more
There was a vow of support for continuing to move forth

There was no doubt in our minds of your great skill
For you are driven and forged by forever steel

The sadness reinforced by the absence of the years once young
Your presence a sideline reminder that you're not gone

Hold strong, be brave and continue to beat like a drum
Life's for living even if you do it with a slow hum

The memories that are stored beneath your hood
Are constant reminders of both the bad and good

The lessons learned during travel worldwide
May someday be told long after you've died

Acceptance that absence is a temporary illusion
This will help to avoid any unnecessary confusion

Weep not for a loss, rejoice in the rain
Smile about the good times and all that remains

The beat up old heart still beats and is true
So does the 55 Chevy engine as a reminder to you

2013

It's ALL about You

You wake up every morning at about eight
demanding your breakfast even when you're running late

You come home after a long night out with your friends
insisting that I not question where you've been

You trample over the yard, destroying the manicured grass
That's when I want to smack you on the head and knock you on your a..

It's all about you
Regardless of what I'm going through

You rant and yell at the kids during your selfish moods
while kicking at the dog and complaining of the dog hair on your fancy shoes

You order steak and wine with your meal as I get water and chicken plain
On the drive home you suggest I eat less because of weight I've gained

It's all about you
No one else matters, it's true

You whistle when a curvy woman walks past as you comment on the view
There is anger when a man looks at me twice, although those times are few

You scrimp on the children's wants and needs telling me to hold back the cost
Yet the sky's the limit on the suits you wear and the car you drive at the family's loss

It's all about you
Nothing less will do

You work in an environment that feeds your ego as everyone knows your name
When you come home, you brag about yourself as you look around and complain

Occasionally, you look at me and ask, "Why don't you smile more?"
It occurs to me how little you listen, because we've had this conversation before

It's all about you
And I realize after all these years, that's nothing new

It's always been ALL about you!

Reaching Out...

Always want to do right
More than you want to be right

Choose to do something today that says you're happy and free
Choose to do something today that says, "I'm happy to be me"

When waking to face a new day, do so with gladness in your heart
Look forward to each day holding yourself together lest you fall apart

Reaching for the stars doesn't have to mean your goals are too far to obtain
Reaching for the stars can mean you work harder for the gain

When you wake each morning, do so looking forward to your day
There is strength in your heart that keeps any negativity away

I've often heard that a lie has some truth, although it is never the cure
Taking a leap into honesty leaves your conscious without stain, simple and pure

There are times when things just aren't going right
... and I want to yell and scream and stomp and fight

Instead I calm and take in a different view
One through which, with the same eyes, I learn what I already knew

I control the outcome of my situation as it evolves
When I'm rational, the problems are much easier for me to solve

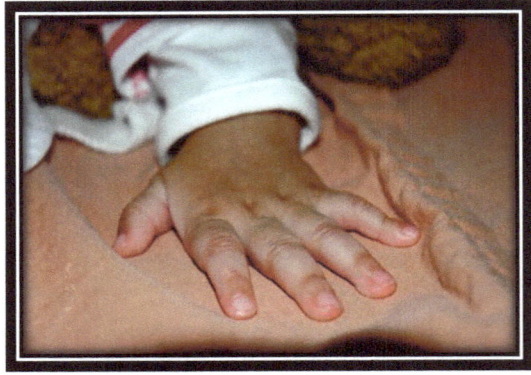

Fight to Survive

My family, friends, and neighbors who care
all want me to know that they are there

If I had a dollar for the many times I said "I want to lose weight"
I dare say I wouldn't be in such a sorry state

Whether it is the food I eat or my lack of exercise
Today I'll change or learn to live with my visible belly and thunder thighs

My leap of faith may provide but a step or two
But, sitting or standing and doing little else doesn't help with what I need to do

It's so easy to sit beneath the tree of woe, watching others bear my burdens of old
Their temporary relief prevents me from looking too closely at my visible folds

During this moment in time, my life is full of gloom
I'm in a dark place, all alone, feeling as though I'm doomed

I look ahead with unchecked tears flowing from my eyes
I see a small light of hope to my wide, self-imposed demise

Whether I walk straight or go round about
I'll latch onto that light and find my way out

When you reach outside of yourself and choose to fight to survive
That is when you learn to appreciate what it takes to be truly alive

I Stand Alone

I stand alone in a crowd of many
knowing life is sparse but there is plenty

I watch and learn
as cigarettes burn

I wonder why, as alcohol is passed around,
no one notices as their changes abound

They laugh, they cry, they argue and fight
but there is not a sound mind to hinder their plight

The fun they sought is rarely seen
as with red eyes, unsteady feet, and slurred speech, they say things they don't mean

I stand back as some become ill
I look away as they seek yet another swill

When is it enough, as the body fights back over time with an ultimate demise?
Is it cancer, cirrhosis of the liver, or other physical changes they cannot disguise?

I hear them say they want to remain among the living
but I watch as they continue to destroy the life they were given

There is always a price for negligence and selfish behaviors by choice
It's difficult to hear or speak when they've drugged or subdued their voice

I stand alone in a crowd of many …
Life is sparse but there is plenty

The Eagle

I wish to fly away and never look back
forgetting all I had and all I lack

It is freedom I seek as my wings expand
with a wish to escape as fast as I can

I'm feeling tired and looking drained
I keep hoping for sunshine and getting rain

I choose to rise to the occasion because of my belief in free will
If we don't work together, our freedom appears less real

I feel saddened by the great divide
What has happened affects most in their pride

If the divide continues, it will be like a lost race
with the enemy within struggling in order to save face

My flight to freedom is short lived and but a dream
as I allow my responsibility to others to draw me to their life streams

There is no easy way out and I choose what makes me feel free
I watch the eagle soar as I return to my own reality

Please Look...and See Me

No, I am not the same person you thought to love … and for that I apologize
I know I hurt you when we were together with my ill-treatment and twisted lies

Instead of treating you with regard and respect
I did the unthinkable, and there is so much that I regret

I watch you now and see how difficult it is for you to accept my apology
I'm sorry for my thoughtless actions, please look … and see me

We both have someone new and have each moved on
Our friendship is fragile as I struggle to make right my wrongs

We have the love of our lives to consider, and he's growing up fast
I'm sorry for my indiscretions; please see me for who I am, not as in the past

I want to make our extended family work for our son's sake and mine
I want to mend the gap between us before we run out of time

He won't be young forever, and we all love him so
When we're together as a family I often feel left out and in the cold

Please look … and see me for who I'm becoming as I change
I'm not perfect with my idiosyncrasies that, I admit, can be a little strange

But I love our son, respect you, your new partner, and mine
Before it was too late, I realized important things last throughout time

Once a Rock

Once a rock, now fine grains of sand
The woman that was never a child, forever changing as she walks the land

Her body fragile and bowed where once it was straight and long
Bowed, but not broken, as she's determined with her will to remain strong

Stitching the wounds caused by a lifetime of tears
She leaves behind the memories that were briefly there

Lost and found she recalls moments of her life as they pass through
Seeing reflections of herself as they appear fresh and new

She questions her own reflection, asking, "Who am I and where have I been?"
If there was no beginning, then there can be no end

Once a rock supporting those she loved without fail
She watches as with the grains of sand, her life is forever unveiled

Today Is a Good Day...

Today is a good day as I look about and smile
Today is a good day with memories of my grandchild

Today is a good day and nothing can make me sadly cry
Today is a good day; sit for a moment and I'll tell you why

Today is a good day; it is your face that does it for me
Today is a good day and I feel so happy and carefree

Today is a good day--see how bright the sun shines
Today is a good day, so pull back the curtains and lift the blinds

Today is a good day; people are out for a walk
Today is a good day and I see their smiles as they talk

Today is a good day; the dog is happy too
Today is a good day with freedom to enjoy all things that you do

Aging

I have no desire to place my life at others' command
I want to be independent for as long as I can

I don't want to have others drop their lives to provide my care
I want to be remembered for my determination and dare

I want to be healthy and to remain strong
I want to be remembered more for what I did right than for what I did wrong

As I age and my body parts gradually fail, I wonder
If I'll be able to hold them together as I ponder

When I was younger, my headaches were from migraines
Now that I'm older, I accept the aches as simply those of life's daily pains

The hair is a little thinner, falling out with each attempt to comb
No complaints as I look around, for I realize I'm not in this alone

My hearing seems to go in and out
But I'm okay, as long as people shout

How dare I get upset at my left eye going blind
I've learned that I'm blessed and able to see just fine

Sensitive teeth and a need for a softer brush
No complaints; at least they're still rooted and strong enough to trust

Oh, the aches and pains that come with getting older
Don't let me get started about my neck and left shoulder

My wrists and ankles crunch and often hurt to the touch
But they remain usable and not uncomfortable (overly much)

(continued...)

(Aging)

My fingers and hands need to be massaged in order to perform with success
The stiffness caused by arthritis has redirected their past efficient progress

My belly has expanded, seemingly with a mind all its own
Its gain in girth requires more food as it places excess weight on aging bones

I once complained about the occasional backache
And now I lean into the discomfort in order to steady my gait

My gluteus maximus was never one to stand out or prompt recall
With aging, it appears to have flattened and not be noticeable at all

The things I once did without a qualm
I now hesitate as my hip slips, causing me alarm

That left knee sure has its days
But no complaints, as it still helps to carry me on my way

My feet hurt and often cramp
Which doesn't do much for me when the weather is damp

Lately my constitution appears to be moving pretty slow
There are days and sometimes weeks when I find it difficult to go

I know that as a baby it was diapers and pampers that we wore
I know that as an aging adult, 'Depends' are now available at the store

The brain is a valuable tool with capacity and a wealth of knowledge available to share
Alzheimer's, dementia, or a stroke could incapacitate the ability to remember what's there

There is the diagnosed status of the inherited disease of the heart
But as long as I keep moving, it'll continue to do it's part

Mother's Day/Father's Day

I love you and I miss you, but I can't stay
I love you and I miss you, but I must be on my way

I love you and I miss you, but we're taking her/his parents to a brunch
I love you and I miss you, maybe next time we'll do lunch

I love you and I miss you, but there's just no time
I love you and I miss you, but I know you're doing fine

I love you and I miss you, tell Mom/Dad I said hi
I love you and I miss you, see you later ... goodbye

I love you and I miss you, being away is sometimes tough
I love you and I miss you, I drove past because the time I had wasn't enough

I love you and I miss you, but I haven't seen my friends in a while
I love you and I miss you, but I'm no longer a child

I love you and I miss you, thanks for all that you did for me
I love you and I miss you, I wish I'd made time to stop and see

I love you and I miss you, I wish you were still here
I love you and I miss you, but all that's left are my tears

I love you and I miss you, I brought flowers from around the old oak tree
I love you and I miss you, all you ever wanted from me was time ... and it was free

Feeling on Top of the World

In order for me to feel on top of the world, I make you feel "less than"
In order for me to feel on top of the world, I respect your role in my life as much as I can

In order for me to feel on top of the world, I make note of all that you do wrong
In order for me to feel on top of the world, I show appreciation for all you've done

In order for me to feel on top of the world, I frown and judge your every comment
In order for me to feel on top of the world, I listen as I accept your message and its intent

In order for me to feel on top of the world, I stay ahead of what you're about to say
In order for me to feel on top of the world, I attempt to learn from my mistakes

In order for me to feel on top of the world, I encourage you to see that my way is right
In order for me to feel on top of the world, I remain open to your thoughts and insight

In order for me to feel on top of the world, I often say mean things with no sense of humility
In order for me to feel on top of the world, I apologize for my selfishness and cruelty

I Believe Success Is Earned

I work hard to succeed, without expectations of fame
I work hard to succeed and to cause my loved ones no shame

I work hard to succeed and to remain humble in my quest
I work hard to succeed and ensure I do my very best

I work hard to succeed and look forward to personal growth
I work hard to succeed and create in life a peaceful flow

I work hard to succeed and it's not about things
I work hard to succeed and hope someday to earn my wings

I work hard to succeed and the path has never been straight
I work hard to succeed and I have yet to know my fate

I work hard to succeed but perhaps the price is too high
I work hard to succeed and to do more than just get by

I work hard to succeed and my dreams are my own to command
I work hard to succeed as I follow through with my plans

58: "Happy Birthday to You"

Age is but a number--
Stand still long enough and you begin to slumber

You recall your aches and pains at 58
You forget your past life, interest, and debates

With age comes thoughts of how things used to be
Of how your once strong eyesight is now fraught with limited ability to see

As you drive slowly, leaning forward into the steering wheel
You remember that once you sat straight, alert, and steady as steel

Age is but a number and 58 is what you've become
It isn't very old, but it isn't very young

It offers you a stage of conquered wisdom
While providing you an opportunity to review the things you've done

Your bones crunch when you stand
Your back is supported by your hands

You grimace with each step
--and frown at your lack of pep

You ask yourself, "What happened to my long ago fast pace--
when I had the strength to give the girls a grand old chase?"

True and Everlasting Friendship

Friendship is a very precious commodity
Filled with joy, pain, love, and offered comradery

It can be as strong as a close family
It can be as lasting as the best relationship history

When friendships are true
Disagreements are worked through

You laugh, smile, cry, yell, and maybe fall apart
You hold each other up as you refresh and restart

Friendship isn't intended for everyone to say "yes"
It's a beautiful interaction that requires many tests

Friendship is not for the faint of heart with little to say
You don't give up on each other or conduct emotional displays

Friendships are a challenge and worth the ordeal
True friendships suffer, but they always rebound and heal

Friendships have a personality, to each its very own
Friendships forever remain, long after the bodies are gone

Friendships create memories to sustain you for when you each return home
Friendships bring out the happiness as you sit alone

(continued...)

(True and Everlasting Friendship)

Friendships are thoughtful and considerate through years of development
Friendships keep you smiling long after your frustrations are spent

Friendships show appreciation for what you each bring to the table
Friendships are understanding, supportive, and helpful when you're not able

Friendship is beautiful, lasting throughout time
True friendship is forever, creating a connection that binds

Friends don't always see eye to eye
Friends don't always agree or choose to take sides

True friends don't allow insignificant gossip to darken their connection
True friends hold onto the heart ties that dictate their secure friendship perfection

My friendships of heart range from 41 years down to less than 2
Each year of friendship is precious, from the many years to the few

True friends in my life leave me feeling whole and blessed
Thanks to you, friends of my heart, I am able to follow my life quest

How Can We Ever Win?

How can we ever win? You have the 36-24-36 body
Everyone thinks you are quite the hottie

You have the long and flowing hair
Sometimes life just doesn't seem fair

Your nails are always manicured and looking nice
They draw attention of others and appear to entice

Your complexion is perfect and a beautiful brown
People seeing you for the first time are often astounded

My complexion is much darker and there was a time I was offered advice
of how to make it beautiful and how to make it light

My nails are short and stubby, with a ragged edge you cannot miss
If they draw the attention of others, I tightly form a fist

My hair is short and tight with no waves and such
I used a hot iron and chemicals to straighten it and soften to the touch

I wore a wig for a time because I thought I needed to hide
this hair that was the butt end of jokes until I began to wear it with pride

My body was thin and slender and I was called "bony rony" in jest
Until I began to grow into this body with a developed butt and chest

I see so many shapes, sizes, hair colors, features, heights, and skin tones about
They are each unique and beautiful regardless of personal concerns and doubts

How can we ever win when the judgements are so cruel and insensitive
Self-acceptance is a start when faced with unrelenting approaches that are negative

I've decided I'll grow into this body and love it at my best
There's something to be said for my still-developing butt and chest

I can't change my skin color that appears to cause some to stare
Since it will always be there, I've decided to accept my tight hair

I'm ok with being myself, although it took time for me to come around
I've accepted that sometimes life just doesn't seem fair, but I won't let it keep me down

2014

My Heart Seeks ... My Mind Incomplete

I reach for something I feel I lack
I listen when you say you love me, as I know you're holding back

There are no riches greater than together spending time
But I feel you distance yourself in heart and in mind

I seek what I have yet to find in whole or in part
Acceptance, understanding, and unconditional love from the heart

It's lonely when you reach the door but find it closed to your request
I stand there hoping to be accepted as I've given you my very best

It seems to never be quite enough when all I do is wrong and I feel defeat
I refuse to give up what my heart seeks as my mind feels incomplete

Forever hopeful that my needs will be known
To be loved as I am with no judgement shown

I am willing to forego the rituals, whatever they may be
If only someone would love, accept, and regard me as they see

I am not perfect, but neither are my flaws so great as to be seen as a lost cause
My heart seeks what my mind feels is incomplete and for that I will give no pause

This is not going to work ... choose not to say
Because giving up and giving in is the easy way

How can I make this happen ... as my mind seeks what my heart feels is incomplete
Choose to work hard to make it last, knowing that to give in is to accept defeat

What Makes You Smile?

Life is but a smile, a single step in time
Leading you forth with an open mind

We each create our joy as we choose to live with purpose and resolute
It's wise to defer to fear as caution, allowing happiness in our hearts as a tribute

Look around you every day and find something that makes you smile
Take any opportunity to view your life as worthwhile

It isn't all bad, unless we make it so
There can be a crack in every window that reveals a little glow

Hold on to that brightness and encourage it to grow in form
If the darkness starts to move in, smile as you move closer to where it's warm

What makes you smile, even when it's raining and gloomy outside?
Thoughts of the garden you planted and the results of your work with pride

What makes you smile, when nothing seems to have gone right?
You know you did your best as you struggled with all of your might

What makes you smile, when you feel everyone has let you down?
The knowledge that you're secure with the inner strength you've found.

This Day Is Your Forever

There is no end to true love and care
You remain together because you choose to be there

You laugh and smile over silly things as they occur
Never lingering too long as together your strength creates a stir

Perfection is not what you sought when you met
Each of you allowed your patience to cast this forever net

The joy I witness as I look into your eyes
reminds me of the glow I feel from a strong sunrise

Each family is gaining a daughter in kind
as you each agree to a partnership that binds

Through your dreams and future plans
Never forget your love as you strive to understand

If ever you look back to see how your lives unfolded
Remain secure in each other's loving hold

There is nothing to keep you from many years of success
So, captain your ship of life and "damn" the rest

9 Against 1

"Faith comes in many forms"
Thought the 9 who attended services, as was their norm

The acceptance of 1 within was who they were
Loss of life wasn't something they believed would ever occur

The numbers are small but the intent is grand
Depend on each other as together you band

9 against 1 from a scale of 10
Leaves room to look forward and not forget where you've been

Who are we to judge those not the same
Faith is in welcoming all without questioning from where they came

Open your arms and your heart if true
Treat others in a manner you hope they will treat you

Approach the problems you face
--with dignity and grace

Live today as if "1" is all that you have to spare
Think not of the "9" that have yet to be there

1 against 9 allows the distance to draw near
You are not alone as you denounce inner fear

I Can't Swim

The water is cold and I tremble inside
Getting out of the pool affects my pride

Ducking beneath the water as I hold my breath in turn
I'm fascinated by the view while sinking in depth as my lungs burn

Is the dizziness and feel of being lightheaded normal to display?
Perhaps I should rise to the surface and live to see another day

I kick like a frog and go nowhere
I move to the side wall and glue myself there

There arises some shame as the 3- and 4-year-olds swim past
I become brave as I watch and tried again at last

Lying on my back making small kicks like a dog
Until I become tired and start floating like a wayward log

My heart is beating fast and my throat starts to burn
I try not to panic as my stomach begins to churn

Determination and willpower change the idea that "I can't swim"
I relax as I kick off the wall on my back and gently move on a whim

I realize that the more I say "I can't swim," the more it impacts my ability
My tactics aren't smooth or perfect at all, but letting go of worry helps me
    to focus on me

Feeling Uncomfortable

I watch you enter the office and continue to stand
I offer you 1 of 3 seats with the gesture of my hand

Dare I say you scare me or hold to confidence I've retrieved?
Dare I turn around without a word and hope for you to leave?

There has been no sign of attack
And yet I refuse to turn my back

Your face displays a frown
Should I be concerned as your thoughts abound?

My skin feels tight with hairs on end
I see your clenched fists and hope not to offend

Your voice is halting and words appear slowed
It's important I appear steady and not like a wide-eyed doe

I watch with patience, not speaking too soon
This allows me the time to analyze and give you plenty of room

We cannot allow my compassion for you and your needs
to prevent me from addressing what you require to root seeds

It is important for me to speak with respect to you
I briefly share my discomfort and ask for your point of view

I silently watch as you sigh, relax your stance, frown, and make a fist
My body freezes as you reach into your pocket and hand me a list

I smile as I read through your past week's progression
I shake my head with empathy as I close out our session

Your physical discomfort is hemorrhoids, which you described in detail with flair
My moments of uncomfortable feelings have nothing on your week of
    painful disrepair

Wait for It...

The common denominator that seems so intelligent
You are cruel and never seem to get the hint

"You have no common sense," I think, as I wait for you to open your mouth
You appear thoughtless as your responses mean little and always go south

I want you to see me as better than I am
Strong as a wolf, not weak as a lamb

Too strong to give up or give in without cause
It helps when you notice things I do right without pause

"Wait for it" ... perhaps that's a setup for every failure as a lead
Positive thoughts and actions speak to the ultimate in time with what will be

"Wait for it," with a smile for the satisfaction of knowing you are appreciated
Walk into the warm welcome of gratitude that supports your desire to challenge what's fated

Give Back

My faith and grace keep me strong
I'm not always right but I'm not always wrong

I refuse to be cocky when life is on track
You never know when you may get knocked on your back

Hold your head high as you're humbled indeed
Reach for the stars as others follow your lead

Give back from your great success
You are never alone in your troubles, lest you forget

When you see others scrambling from the bottom to reach the top
Offer a helping hand to gift them the opportunity someone else may not

Open your eyes and don't be blind
It takes little for you to simply be kind

There are those that see their large incomes and material gains, saying "I have arrived"
Don't be among those, as they limit their abilities to give back and help others
    to survive

Self-Acceptance

She had the audacity to be born a dark-complexioned black woman, with little to no leverage
Her tight kinky hair belies any questions of her definitive heritage

She defies the expected by having an intelligent mind
Which appears to shock those seeking ignorance from her and her kind

She displays large brown eyes with short fringed lashes that are curly and dark
There's no missing her appearance, which stands out so stark

She has a tiny, noticeable little button nose
Which appears deep red when it becomes cold

She has in sync lips that are full and sure
There's no mistaking her generous smile with its patience endured

She has a heartfelt tendency to care enough to speak out on behalf of others
This denotes her self-preservation when seeing all as her fellow sisters and brothers

She accepts the repercussions when there's a lack of appreciation for her interventions
It doesn't stop her from doing the same again, all with good intentions

She feels like a perfectly filleted salmon left open to the elements
in preparation for cooking and later consumption with a calm that has no precedent

She appears to have little acceptance of any form of prejudice and pride
Choosing, instead, to believe that all have rights, with ethnicity and color aside

She feels that all are different and unique as their features show
Qualifications as individuals begins with the self-acceptance, they know

She doesn't think the color of her skin determines who she is or will be
She's hopeful that someday, everyone will connect and feel secure in their Individuality

Sweet Ollie

Those big, beautiful brown eyes can't help but draw you in
That sweet smile makes you want to hug and squeeze him again and again

Eyes so much older than his young years
Carrying a conversation for listening ears

Just a small child with a wise old soul
Speaking unexpected words, loud and bold

Many are surprised at his ability
To follow what is said while in adult company

He's watchful of what others communicate
Giving voice to what he appears to relate

Such a wise child with an age-old soul
With the beginning of a knowledge to be strengthened and molded

He has a lightness of heart that reaches out to those needing help
Seeking to calm them with little understanding of their painful steps

Sweet Ollie is smart and observant, but still a child
With years remaining to reinforce his wisdom with a joyous smile

2015

Difficult to Explain

I have many wounds, cuts, bruises, and breaks
None of which were given or made by mistake

The damage leaves visible scars, some shallow and some deep
Once the harm is done, I'm able to finally get some sleep

I often dream of being on a beach, experiencing the calm
I am reminded that my pain is temporary ... and yet still I self-harm

As the waves flow in gently and wash away the sand, they leave behind
Small creatures struggling to return to the waters, away from the bright sunshine

I watch as I make plans for the day
--feeling thoughtful because I decided to stay

Sometimes life is like a pretense to live
Inside I think I'll die again tomorrow, while believing I have little to give

I don't need drugs or any other escapes from the edge of a knife
When I focus on living, I become high on life

I want to share with others and convince them I'm someone they need to know
But why talk about my life if I have nothing to show?

While looking at my mother as she complains and talks about wanting to bail
I wish to shout my conscious thoughts and have her acknowledge me in detail

It is difficult to explain why I self-harm and physically scar my skin
There is little understanding of emotions deeply bound, once suffused within

(continued...)

(Difficult to Explain)

It helps to address and attempt to sort out the pain
But too often, I return to that place I feel keeps me sane

I know what I do to myself and desperately want to heal
But, it's difficult to explain triggers as they reset my need to feel

I'm slowly learning to live one day at a time
Although it is difficult to explain, I know I am of sound mind

I must reach beyond the great seeds of doubt
This is a fight for my life from the inside out

It is difficult to explain, and I know I'm not alone or wrong
If we are to survive the pain, we must first learn to be strong

Some Want Them

Some want them but cannot have them
Some have them but do not want them

They are vulnerable in any form
They trust without pause because it is their norm

Are they always perfect ... No, it's true
But what are they learning as they watch and mimic you?

Love is a given until there's a mistake
Followed by yelling, profanity, and aggressive words of hate

The emotional pain and hurt is real as tears easily flow
They learn to harden their hearts because there's no place for them to go

Who will believe children when an adult shows sincere regret?
Who will listen to their voice when they are young yet?

Their eyes watch as their ears listen to lies that unfold
Who will believe they speak the truth once the adult's story is told?

The innocence is departing as their number in age does increase
Through the eyes and ears of time, their truth, once told, will now cease

Dare they make use of the profanity and abuse so often heard at home?
Are the streets a better place to be than a place where they feel alone?

They didn't ask to be born or to be placed in your care
Why can't you find it in your heart to love them once they are there

Love is not a check to elicit a smile of joy temporarily, leaving little else behind
Love is sought as a permanent source of comfort for them over their lifetime

Believe...

Believe in yourself when you think no one else will
Don't negate your faults--instead, look closer at your skills

Why tear yourself down when you'll have to rebuild
Look closer at your heart and choose reasons to live

Life is not easy when death is tempting and strong
The permanence of death is a reminder of why taking a life is wrong

It's the monster inside
--that makes you want to hide

All the more reason for you to come out and play
--to live for tomorrow but stay alive for today

Look for reasons to hope for a cause
Learn to love yourself without hesitation or pause

Feel that you're worthy and be confident in yourself
Feel the essence of your life and hold true to what's left

Believe that you're stronger than you realize
Take time to plan your future and open wide your eyes

There is more to you than a number, age, position, looks, or beautiful mind
You're unique as an individual and only one of a kind

The Bug

It didn't come at me with sneezing, coughing, or runny nose as is the trend
Instead, it was silent as it slowly descended

Two weeks of belly aches, nausea, and a declining appetite
I didn't see it coming as it took baby chunks and small bites

The headaches and dizzy spells slowly came to pass
I thought I could handle things, believing nothing forever lasts

Seeing life as but a single step in time, when approached openly
Knowing that we each attend our health with an interest in what life can be

It is wise to defer to fear as a mere means of precaution until the process is done
But allow the doctor to determine if the bug is a serious one

Although it's lasting a while and is a drain on your energy
It isn't permanent and with rest and care, you'll soon be back on your feet

Don't panic when the bugs creep in, setting you on edge
Relax as your body heals and make a future pledge

The bug is like a visitor that arrives unannounced
Remaining when you're not prepared, taking the opportunity to pounce

Plan for any future returns with the appropriate and necessary medications
The bug doesn't have a chance to stay with managed self-care and preparation

You Are a Wonder

You are a wonder and a treasure to many whose paths you have crossed
Your venture into the life you've chosen will leave a void, but not a complete loss

I'll have memories of your smiling face
and thoughts of the artful way you'd often create without haste

In the beginning, I realized the special young lady you were to become
It's with sincere pleasure that I continue to believe you have yet much to be done

I believe you are whole and complete in your resolution to succeed
Congratulations, young lady, as you move forward to wherever your dreams
    may lead

Patience Resolves Much

It may not be today, as is your intent
Tomorrow will be soon enough; relax and don't over-vent

Yelling and raising your voice
Never helps, and limits your choice

Give what you have to offer, no more and no less
There is a good feeling when you know you've done your best

Why hurry when you may miss something along the way?
Take your time, making note of the sights on display

Hold yourself to a standard which others seek to follow
Allow yourself to treasure each moment, leaving no room for sorrow

Patience resolves much, especially if your health is on the line
Remember, you'll get to where you're going, it may just take a little more time

Who Am I That I Care?

That I beat the odds and look for better too occur
That my life provides challenges as it passes in a blur

That I feel secure in who I perceive myself to be
That my choices leave me open to explore my own eternity

That I believe in God's influence on my life
That I thrive in peace and avoid anything causing strife

That I care so deeply for others and their pain
That I tend to reach out, with no interests in personal gain

That I sense strongly the emotions, an open floodgate
That my heart is filled to capacity knowing it's never too late

That I refuse to feel hopeless and helpless overly long
That when I see darkness, I know the light will keep me strong

That I defend the underdog and speak up for those in doubt
That my empathy isn't subtle, instead more of an audible shout

That I watch you and gauge your response with an open mind
That even when you are ruthless, my treatment of you remains kind

That I want everyone to do more than just guess or try
That I have faith in humanity for truths without lies

That I want to give my very best ...
That in my heart you will always be an honored guest

Share Your Thoughts

Share your thoughts, you know not all
Think of how you feel when life seems to stall

Share your thoughts, be discreet in what you say
Life is full of mystery which unfolds from day to day

Share your thoughts, don't be afraid
Search your mind for distant memories, present though vague

Share your thoughts, full and free they spread
Grasp what you believe to be true as it floats inside your head

Share your thoughts, they reveal how much you care
Some of life you were missing, but for much of it you were there

Share your thoughts, never minimize your part
You are appreciated for all stored within your heart

Share your thoughts, knowing you can never take anyone's place
Recall things that are meaningful, accepting none of it as waste

Share your thoughts, they are precious in time
Know that it's your love which strengthens, helping to make everything fine

Share your thoughts, never giving up or giving in
Hold true to your emotions as select family and friends

Share your thoughts, you played a crucial role
In the trials of this life as it continues to unfold

Share your thoughts, I await your feelings and review
Let go and let God ... I have faith in you

2016

Woke Up Today

I woke up today
Unsure of what to say

Quiet, solemn, and silent still
Considering the day as it slowly filled

Never a moment to stop and relax
Sorting the challenges and reviewing the facts

Housework and chores, they never seem to end
The responsibilities ... too numerous to contend

Not wanting to stop once the need to follow through starts
Feeling overwhelmed as I emotionally begin to fall apart

Focused on completing the tasks without creating a mess
Letting go of the desire to stop and rest

Never regret taking the first step
To do something meaningful without expecting help

Lying down for hours and watching time pass
Is not an option if I am to last

As I proceed through the day, I begin to smile and sing
Pleased to have awakened to the joys my life brings

Pain

You wish for death
You try to turn and lose your breath

You pray for God's relief
You cry inside with disbelief

You wish to blackout
You release an involuntary shout

You feel nauseous and want to throw up with no reason of why
You hold back the urge, seeking control as time passes by

You feel devastated, like you're going insane
You realize that with every movement there is increased pain

You lie there for 18 hours believing you can get up and move
You refuse to accept your situation and that you have nothing to prove

You plead not to be touched
You think … "Oh God, this is too much"

You're willing to accept "anything" to take the pain away
Your thoughts about drugs, for the first time ever, begin to sway

You feel like you're lost in the darkest of times
You believe you'd rather die than keep losing your mind

You beg and plead for the pain to go away
You lie there with hope as it continues to stay

You hesitate when the doctor says to reproduce what you feel
You dread the oncoming results but do as he wills

(continued…)

(Pain)

You shout and reach for his gut as the pain returns with force
Your tears flow unchecked as the doctor looks on with remorse

You listen as you're told the bulging disc in your back is bad
You lie in pain as the variety of drugs wear off, leaving you feeling sad

You are disillusioned after three medication tries, feeling doubt and grief
You cry, thinking nothing will help as the fourth medication finally brings relief

You feel as if you've levitated from the bed during the steroid injections
Your tears flow freely as you squeeze fingers of an angel nurse who reveals
    no objections

You are relieved the following day, but fearful of what your future holds
You appear unsure as your results reveal you may have new and challenging roles

You accept your life change and limited options in turn
You pray to live with all of the lessons you've learned

You know that the passing of the pain has no guarantees
You acknowledge your life and health to be your personal responsibility

You look at your life anew, the traumatic pain seeming unreal
You believe yourself blessed to be walking and for your body's ability to heal

You view the pain as an experience you hope to never feel again
You find yourself waking each day in prayer as you proceed to stand

You hope to never take advantage of being able to simply get out of bed
You work daily to conquer fear and thoughts of the pain left behind within your head

Naysay and Meaningless Chatter

Nothing is right when everything spoken is wrong
Why bother speaking when you can silently sing a song?

You wait to speak and to be heard
knowing your listener will naysay your every word

Perhaps if you research your topic, their response will change
No, now you're a "know-it-all" and your retorts are strange

Asking questions appears to solicit a face that says you annoy
Saying nothing elicits questions about your lack of joy

Occasionally, you smile, knowing the naysay will come
Regardless of your topic, once you've begun

Meaningless chatter to occupy the space of silent retreat
Receives a look of disappointment meant to cause defeat

A facial frown intended to draw you down
Provides time to rethink in preparation to rebound

The feeling of hurt and loss is temporary but true
Letting go when there is naysay helps put things in perspective for you

The need for meaningless chatter is of personal intent
Don't be offended when the response lacks understanding of what was meant

Be okay with what you say if it causes others not to hurt
Don't waste your life wondering, when cross words create hard work

Longtime Friends

Friends have no flag that separates color
They are simply there in support of each other

Each has a right to what they believe or say
What others may think doesn't affect them or cause a parting of ways

A particular race or ethnic group does not draw the line
The truth of heartfelt friendship lasts beyond the end of time

A couple of friends entered an establishment to get out of the weather
They were approached and asked, "Are the two of you together?"

… Yes, they cautiously said
… as both began to nod their heads

"I couldn't help but notice a Confederate flag on your hat"
The friends looked at each other, finding nothing wrong with that

One said to the patron, "I don't give a s… about his politics
--he's got the boat and I'm going to catch some fish"

Fishing

Fishing is not for the faint of heart
It requires patience and calm from the start

The fish do not come easily as they fight to be free
Your strength against their will to live determines what will be

Fish do not lie in wait to be caught
The struggle to reel them in is a battle to be fought

Sometimes it takes a day or more to get one on the hook
Reminding you that the process is not as simple as it looks

The fish flops back and forth when removed from its watered home
Once it's been knocked senseless, the fight is all but gone

Watching a group of people standing side by side
Casting their fishing lines and taking life in stride

No one appears in a hurry
Temporarily they've set aside their worries

The hours seem to slowly pass
while people talk and continue to cast

The tide comes in, covering the low dock with the water's gentle flow
The fishermen move to higher ground but none choose to go

There are nearly 100 people fishing at the fishing hole
Many standing tall and sure as they draw back their fishing poles

Everyone knows the best way to cast and catch a fish
It makes your mouth water, thinking of the soon-to-be-cooked dish

The fish gives its life for you to have your meal
It's important to give thanks since you get the better end of the deal

Respect and Regard

Serving your country, state, or community because it feels right to you
Belief in your heart that it's the important thing to do

Giving little thought to the possible inevitable end
Holding true to the need to protect and defend

You've earned the right for respect and regard
You didn't ask to be noticed for working so hard

Each day, you place your life on the line
Never knowing the outcome of what you'll find

Some that made the same choice as you
Neglect their vow to protect and defend in truth

Although they are not the majority, being instead the few
It's their irresponsible behaviors that often make the news

There is no limit to what you're willing to achieve
Your selfless treatment of others fulfills a necessary need

Male or female matters not
When in the field you give all you've got

Your uniform comes in many colors and designs
Thank you for your service and commitment of your time

For those that are active, leaving, or retired
None mean less than the other, given the young you inspire

Respect and regard to you and your uniform of choice
It is because of you that I have the freedom of voice

See, But Don't Be Seen

See, but don't be seen
Invisibility is not a viable go-between

Listen, but don't be heard
Continue to hear as you formulate your own words

Have voice, but don't speak
Never give up on the words you seek

Struggle to walk, but stand alone
Believe someone is there to help keep you strong

Reach for the stars, but pull away
Fear breeds doubt, there is hope when you pray

Aware of scents, but refuse to smell
Odor without cleanliness eventually tells

Believe you can, but never try
Life's for living with no time to die

Feel your worth and let faith be your stand
Believe you will succeed even without a plan

Death Called

Death called, removing warmth while bringing cold
And yet she survived with a beautiful soul

Her smiles are bright and joy sincere
She's pleasing to watch with her motives so clear

Honesty, with a free spirit that shines
Drawing others to her presence and heart so kind

Cancer tried to take her life more than a single time
It was through the grace of God that she lengthened her life's line

She prayed for strength as she held true to her code
Unsure of her future as her life unfolded

The mother of three and wife full of love
Refusing to die or ever give up

Feeling the need to stay healthy and secure
In her belief that God would provide a cure

Considerate and thoughtful to the needs of others
Always striving to better understand their life struggles

Although she had nothing to prove
She agreed to a long-distance move

Questions were there
… but she didn't seem to care

(continued…)

(Death Called)

Her decision to "Let go and let God" became her guide to being alive
Leading her on a journey of appreciation that she is strong enough to survive

When she looks back at those she left behind
Her heart fills with love, knowing they will be fine

She'll return to their fold
… to resume her loving role

… of mother, sister, daughter, and friend, to those she helped to ground
Her absence having strengthened them during the times she wasn't around

Short in stature, with a wealth of height to spare
Wearing her heart on her sleeve and showing how much she cares

Feeling grateful to God for bringing her to me
Her encouragement helping to push me to be active and healthy

Many blessings are open to interpretation
Acceptance of the gift of "Her" is reason for celebration

Death called, but she did not heed
Instead plotting her future with life as her lead

Feeling Pushed Over the Edge

So overwhelmed until you can barely breathe
Wanting to stay while wanting to leave

Holding back and pushing down emotions that are so strong
Needing the release but feeling it's wrong

Hearing the faceless voice over the phone
Feeling saddened by the seemingly angry tone

Distraught and feeling pushed over the edge
Sliding to the floor in a corner where you're wedged

Sitting in the corner while crying your heart out
Finally letting go, letting loose a heart-wrenching shout

Accepting your façade of life as having been a mere illusion
Disavowing your beliefs of fairness has instilled more confusion

Releasing your painful rose-colored glasses as you give up the fight
Just because you wanted it, doesn't mean everyone will treat you right

Never allow your hurt to run too deep to control
Take steps each day of life to maintain the purity of your soul

Crying, yelling, screaming in pain as you reach down deep
… does nothing more when upset than interfere with sleep

(continued…)

(Feeling Pushed Over the Edge)

Feeling pushed over the edge when a sound mind says compromise
Relax your heart as with each automatic response you improvise

Believe in yourself and the ability to look disappointment in the eye
Never give so much that it elicits the involuntary need to cry

Stop and breathe, taking each situation in stride
Remain in the present and salvage your pride

Sort through the anguish and lingering despair
Realize the potential to be the better person will always be there

Tomorrow brings fresh insight and renewed hope
Accept that you're capable of learning to cope

No, Leo...

Leo, the baby lion of a year
Seeks to challenge authority without fear

Running in circles while laughing with glee
Watching the response of all that could see

Flittering about with mischief in mind
Sweeping everything from the tables that he finds

Running away from those giving chase
Looking over his tiny shoulder with a smile on his face

Stopping just long enough to get into trouble
When someone says, "No, Leo," his escape efforts are doubled

His stubby little legs appear to stumble with the extra effort to run
His bright grey-green eyes shine with enjoyment and fun

There is no letting up as Leo chooses another route
You hear something crash followed by a "No, Leo" shout

Leo's big brother Ollie says, "Come see what Leo did over there"
There's no need to hurry as Leo awaits my entrance with his grey-green-eyed stare

He makes no effort to get away and hide
Standing strong, looking at his destruction with pride

(continued...)

(No, Leo ...)

Leo takes off again while I'm cleaning his latest break
His big brother following closely in his wake

You smile as you hear "No, Leo " and prepare to confront a new mess to clean
Without speech or verbal communication, Leo's grunts and finger-pointing reveal the next scene

"Look, Grandma, he broke your angel and he wouldn't listen to me"
For the first time Leo stops as he looks at the broken angel at my feet

The angel is in pieces but Leo is fine, with no cuts to be seen
"It's okay, Leo, Grandpa can fix it, but you have to stop breaking Grandma's things"

The look on his fallen face appears to show regret, upon close inspection
Just as he smiles, taking off again and running in a new direction

While removing the broken glass, I hear "No, Leo" with an effort towards interruption
A new smile upon my lips, I seek the newest "Leo" destruction

Finally, it's lunchtime and Leo loves to eat
He calms as he tires soon after, falling fast asleep

Black Man Running

Why do you run?
I run because it's an activity I enjoy
I experience the freedom that comes with the energy I deploy

Why do you run?
I fear the disbelief my innocence entails
The color of my skin will not allow me to prevail

Why do you run?
My guilt is a given, although I've done no wrong
To respond that I'm innocent could cause someone to draw their gun

Why do you run?
The fear that is evident and running through me so true
... is the same fear that I know occasionally runs through you

Why do you run?
Leaving the scene of a crime in which I did not partake
I'm running like there's no tomorrow, knowing it's a mistake

Why do you run?
After coming upon the scene and being unsure of what to do
I look for a way out, only to get caught without a clue

Why do you run?
She pointed a finger and said I looked like the man she'd seen
The officer glanced my way and said I needed to come clean

(continued...)

(Black Man Running)

Why do you run?
I made a mistake while a young man, leading to a warrant for my arrest
If they catch me now, I'll become their incarcerated guest

Why do you run?
The uniform reminds me of when my dad got shot
There was so much blood that I never forgot

Why do you run?
My mom says to "do as they say and they'll let you go"
But I'd watched as they'd brutally cuffed my innocent best friend Joe

Why do you run?
Unsure of being shot, even with my raised hands
I'm shaking so hard it makes me feel like less of a man

Why do you run?
I know they're not all bad and I have police friends in the field
But there are the few who seem to relish in the "black man kills"

Why do you run?
I want to be treated fair with respect, regard, and dignity
But I run without thought because I fear I may not remain free

Why do you run?
I'm frightened of what they might see
The color of my skin works against me

Holding Hands

They walk at a leisurely pace
Watching each other with a shy grace

They are old enough to understand
... their special connection as they hold hands

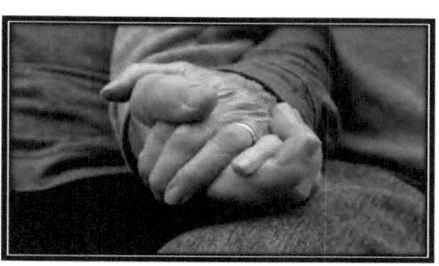

He opens the car door to help her in
... securing her seat belt with a kiss to her chin

Smiling as he walks around to take a seat
... winking at her once he's in the car, away from the heat

She holds his hand and kisses his cheek
... saying, "Thank you, my love, for such a grand feat."

Holding hands while driving slowly and talking in comradery
"It's been 40 years, but my heart still knows you're a part of me"

The need to touch each other is strong
They gravitate toward one another as the years pass along

Much of their communication is silent but for a smile
There's little need for words when you've been together for awhile

Holding hands each Sunday when attending church
Making eye contact as they thank God they met each other first

Holding hands as they wait for God to call him home
Knowing she'll soon follow and not be left alone

Daydreaming about the love of her life while turning her wedding band
Thinking of the many times he made her feel special when holding hands

Preparing to say goodbye to loved ones, knowing she can no longer stay
Feeling him holding her hands and waiting patiently for her to slip away

Winding Roads

waiting to see around the next curve
so fearful as I shake with nerves

unsure of oncoming traffic
praying to remain steady to avoid getting hit

the beautiful scenery leaves me in awe
of the life experienced so tranquil and raw

winding roads to surprise you with all you see
bringing out the most to sustain my memory

dare I take my eyes from the path
chancing an accident that may affect my enjoyment so vast

the roads are full of straight lines without breaks
there can be no passing, leaving room for mistakes

so much to look at and appreciate
wanting to take it all in before it's too late

the pullovers and turnoffs give you leave to enjoy
the many sites off the road under nature's employ

fallen rocks, gravel, sand and debris
take nothing away from the endless beauty

winding roads with treats that please …
I'm grateful for the memorable opportunities

Tennessee Sisters

They talk with a smile filled with animation
Their connection is observed through their elation

They appear happy and content in the company of each other
It's beautiful to watch them as they support one another

They discuss their lives past and present
Their memories of clarity with life events

Sisters that smile and show their grace
So many similarities revealed in their face

What a precious thing to behold
These sisters together, sharing their lives as it unfolds

They hug and look each other in the eyes
There are no secrets between the sisters to hide

Their lives have had challenges and trials of trust
Yet they stand strong because they know they must

These sisters are aware that their lives lack perfection
Watching them express their love reinforces their forever connection

North Pole Santa

He has a happy laugh and a smile that shines
With a welcome feeling that surpasses time

He hugs all as they arrive with glee
Giving each individual an experience that's free

He listens to every gift request
Assuring the owner of his full attention and nothing less

He gets great delight from those with special needs
Squeezing them tight as his emotions exceed

North Pole Santa with his beard so white
His sincere smile paving the way so bright

What a grand gesture with his rosy cheeks
North Pole Santa with his "jolly physique"

He gives insight into what could be for all
The willingness to love openly, without finding fault

North Pole Santa, it was a pleasure to meet face-to-face
We look forward to Christmas and your return in haste

What a treat to watch individuals of every age
Undertake an opportunity to be photographed with you unfazed

North Pole Santa, these memories are on instant recall and a repeat tread
Smiles you brought to a special young lady are a forever picture in our heads

A Child's Prayer

Please don't let her beat me ... I'll be good
The tears flowing heavily as I stood

Wringing my hands as I looked toward the sky
Begging God to help her see the truth wasn't a lie

The belt over her shoulder as she briefly walked away
My fear that she wouldn't believe anything I had to say

Her return with words I never thought to hear
Listening closely as I wiped away my tears

"This time, I won't beat you for getting into trouble
...but the next time, you will get double"

I think I was in shock as I walked to my room
Afraid she'd come after me and take away my boon

The sky looked brighter and I felt God's presence
Perhaps he'd intervened, holding her hand back in my defense

That was the day I first believed I wasn't alone
Although I couldn't see him, my fear of her wasn't as strong

She'd never threatened to beat me and not followed through
There were many beatings after that, some of which I was due

I'll never forget that day and my prayer ...
God opened my heart, showing me that he was there

Goodbye

Your inviting eyes and open smile
Helped ease my life when I was but a child

I didn't feel judged or less than
When you spoke so that I could understand

I feel blessed that I visited you before God called you home
He knows when the time is right to reconnect before you're left alone

I believe I got to know your heart to be true
Never once did I doubt your acceptance as my due

You saw intelligence in my big, sad eyes
When others saw a dark-skinned child they grew to despise

You listened when I talked and heard what I said
I'll always be grateful for your level head

Knowing that you're gone hurts my heart so deep
But God has you in his hands as you forever sleep

There is no more pain or need to cry out
Only that beautiful smile that I was talking about

When I discovered the time you breathed your last
I understood my emotional need to weep and crash

There was a strong urge to cry out loud
With no explanation for what that was about

I feel calm and at peace now that I know
You'd messaged my spirit as you finally let go

Rest in Peace

Have All of the Answers

Leaving little to chance and fate
Believing in self as you wait

They haven't lived your life and don't really know
Why you distance yourself everywhere you go

Have all of the answers? ... No, not I
There are more questions than answers to live by

Curious about all yet to be learned
Hopeful for the right response when it's your turn

Doubtful of self because of what others might say
Thoughts and beliefs often held at bay

Reaching for answers to fill curiosity shown
Partial response to what is all but known

Have all of the answers and know everything
There is more to be gained simply by listening

Ask me a question and watch as I try
To provide the answers in truth without telling a lie

Wanting to talk to you and communicate
Throwing caution to the wind as we debate

Have all of the answers? ... No, not I ...
There are more questions than answers for us to live by

It Was But A Whisper in My Ear

Did you call to me from your heart?
I heard your outcry from the start

Were you lonely and feeling lost?
I wanted to reach out to you at all costs

What were your tears a reminder of?
I'm here now and you are loved

Why were you sitting so far away?
I want you closer and willing to stay

When did you decide to ask for my help?
I've been here all alone, walking beside you, step by step

Where would you like to start sharing your pains?
Your life is an open book to me and there is no shame

How can you not see that I'm always there?
I patiently await your call to share

Why keep your own counsel when there is choice?
My response to you is action, often without voice

It was but a whisper in my ear
But I knew I no longer needed to shed a tear

Travel to See Wonders of Nature

Travel by foot with few miles to cover
Seeing nature's bounty with much to discover

Travel by bike in the wind and breeze
Seeing and feeling through the windblown trees

Travel by car or truck, enclosed away from the elements
Seeing through the windows but missing nature's scent

Travel by bus with others to discuss your experience
Seeing through their eyes and yours via a multi-faceted lense

Travel by plane to places far away
Seeing their wonders while enjoying the stay

Travel by rail on the trains of thunder
Seeing much nature has to offer in all its wonders

Travel by motorhome in comfort and luxury without worry
Seeing wonders of nature while moving with no need to hurry

Travel by thought with an open mind and free will
Seeing all nature has to offer while standing still

Shower Cry

The shower cry brings water mixed with tears
There is no one to witness the drowning fears

You stand beneath the water and release heartfelt hurts
Watching as they flow down the drain like washed-away dirt

The shower cry is not a sight for the weak of heart
There's often a runny nose and deep emotional noise as the crier falls apart

The shower cry happens when all alone
Lasting until the deep need to cry is all but gone

The shower cry is intended to help ease the pain
Taking time to be rid of the built-up life stains

From day to day, when disappointments abide
The shower cry helps to put them aside

Start each day finding new joy to begin
Let the shower cry at night release any heavy burdens

The shower cry is to self-appease
Providing individual therapy that can take you to your knees

Shower cry ... it's okay
Take advantage at the end of each day

Old But Useful

They seem to believe I'm unable to help
Taking opportunities away from me at every step

I love to drive but their trust has declined
To allow me at the wheel, thinking they're being kind

Cooking is an enjoyable task
But with well-meaning intervention, that doesn't last

The grandbabies are heaven and mischievous in kind
They believe I might have a heart attack, leaving them behind

I feel an urge to purchase simple memories
But am told they already have plenty

Some babies are heavy, putting a strain on the heart
I can still bend these rickety knees with a little help on their part

I'm told not to lift these bundles of joy
The bulging disc in my back a painful decoy

Kisses and smooches I have plenty of
They're great for letting them know how much I love

They are all sweet and loving and I know them well
I take it in stride, hoping they can tell

Old but useful and willing to be there …
Until unable to do for them as much as I'd care

Smiles of Joy

There are smiles of joy that we all seek
Some sought in the face of those in defeat

Because they're feeling doubt as they fall to their knees
You want to make them smile and celebrate what they did achieve

It's easy to draw down when missing the goal of intent
Smiles of joy can remind us of our accomplishments

Think of what you did, not of loss versus gain
Smile with grace and gratitude, not a frown of disdain

Be happy for the steps taken and for not standing still
Through smiles of joy, your life is fulfilled

Hugs and kisses bring warm feelings inside
Making room for acceptance of strength with unbridled pride

Let smiles of joy and happiness abound
When hardships and difficult times are around

Change what you can, letting go of the rest
Smiles of joy will help keep you at your best

The sincere feeling of "I've got this"
Support the smiles of joy you cannot dismiss

It's often your smile that is seen by others
As a reminder of their life and manageable struggles

Smiles of joy are uplifting, and although they're not a fix-all
They can help when someone perceives their life is spiraling into a downward fall

The Suburban, 1980 to 1997

We needed something large with a feeling of safety
Because of our concerns as parents of two new babies

Saw the Suburban sitting in the corner of the lot
Decided it was perfect for the family I've got

The creamy color wasn't fancy or cute
But it was the only vehicle on the lot I felt would do

There was a lot of future traveling in our plans
This was the vehicle destined to meet our demands

The center of the floor was hot enough to heat the baby's food while on the road
The Suburban was strong enough to carry our basic needs in a single load

The twins were potty trained, making it a game among toys they lacked
Climbing over the bench seat to use the portable potty in back

There was room enough for 6 to sleep
With no complaining of two babies between and two on the bench seat

Memories of the dog getting sick from the Suburbans' motion
Followed closely by the oldest child throwing up and mom's heaving notions

Camping overnight with fishing poles in tow
The Suburban a sure thing for a family on the go

Watching in the mirror as my son went flying through the air
When hitting the brakes hard as traffic suddenly slowed while leaving the state fair

It took a few stitches for that little facial repair
The seatbelt removal was a lesson learned for him there

Off to high school they all went
Driving the Suburban they'd all grown up in

The lack of oil for the engine was the final turn
Our family Suburban gone, donated to the fire department for their practice burns

There Is No Win, Only Hurt and Misery

Cowering in the corner as the cruel words tear you apart
Your arms across your chest, as if trying to protect your heart

Feeling the tears flow as you make not a sound
Avoiding his eye contact as you wait for the next round

Trying to think of a time when you felt strong
Wondering what is happening and what you did wrong

Comparing this life to the one you once had
Wanting this one to be better because the other one was bad

Looking straight ahead at the wavering wall
Getting up from the floor as you stand tall

Walk into the room, never saying a word
Pack your meager belongings as if you've never heard

… All the cruel things that've been said and done
That have finally broken you down as you realize he has finally won

You leave wishing him well, knowing your love will always be
Feeling sorry for his blind and controlling nature preventing him from being able to see

There's no coming back from this hurt and misery
His anger has suppressed his once beautiful personality

About the Author

Writing began as a form of escape for me from the world of reality, allowing for self-expression while I lived in a foster home with my siblings and many other children. Some of the poems were written without thought, while others were written as a form of communication without the element of verbal interaction. The poems weren't always about anything or anyone specific.

I grew up learning and believing that children weren't always meant to be seen or heard, so I learned to be creative in my invisibility while hiding in plain sight. My poetry allowed me an "out" in order to somehow feel connected to something during frequent periods of aloneness.

I have lived in Alaska with my beautiful family for over 27 years. I have a husband of over 40 years and together we have, among our extended family, six beautiful adult children and six grandchildren.

www.ingramcontent.com/pod-product-compliance
Lightning Source LLC
Chambersburg PA
CBHW041535220426
43663CB00002B/39